Defying Death

Dr Kathi Perry

Contents

My Personal Journey...1

"One Stop Body Shop" 6

My Approach to Health and Wellness 9

You Are What You Eat and Drink..13

Three Steps to Wellness...19

Taking Care of Your Physical Body...and Mind......................25

Transforming Your Health Through LifeLines..........................28

Infinite Love and Gratitude..38

A Message from Dr. Kathi 42

My Personal Journey

I'm Dr. Kathi Perry. I was born in Kansas, but for the past 30 years I've lived in Texas. An old saying in Texas is "I wasn't born here, but I got here as fast as I could." And I'm glad I got to Texas as fast as I could as the journey has been very good for me.

So many of my patients and other people ask me "how did you get into alternative healthcare, and why?" Well, my story goes back to when I was a little girl in Kansas.

I grew up in a family that really believed in alternative health care which included chiropractic. I can remember having a sore throat or sneezing and my parents would whisk me off to the chiropractor to get adjusted. My family has always approached healthcare proactively, and used natural remedies before going to an allopathic doctor or taking drugs.

As an aside of that, I managed to keep my tonsils until I was about 18 years old. I did have recurrent bouts with strep throat though, so when I was about to go off to college I asked my parents if I could have my tonsils out. Since then I have never had strep throat, but boy that was the worst three weeks of my life recovering from the surgery! Because of that, I learned to be proactive with my health. Now 61, I've only been in the hospital three times during my life: once for my tonsillectomy, once for childbirth and once to have a cyst removed from my Fallopian tube—that was thought to be an ectopic pregnancy.

My mother also worked on us as part of our holistic healthcare. She was a reflexologist and as a child, instead of bedtime stories, I sat in the recliner and got my feet done every night. The whole body is represented on the feet as well as in other areas of the body, so by applying pressure on the different points of the feet, you can help alleviate different issues. While my Mom is not here to work on my feet, if I don't feel well or if I'm stressed out, my husband will rub my feet and I'll feel better and more relaxed.

Another thing my mother taught me was "we are what we eat". We lived in the country where Mom always had an organic garden long before it was popular and we never used inorganic insecticides. If my mother saw an insect on a plant, she'd simply pick it off, put the insects in the blender with some water and soap, and then use that mixture to spray on her plants. She recycled organic waste and used her compost pile as organic fertilizer. Everything was organic.

My mother grew up in the Depression so we canned all of the wonderful food that grew in her garden; we rarely bought anything at the store. One of the things that apparently they didn't have a lot of in the Great Depression was toilet paper so we always had a huge amount of toilet paper in reserve that she would buy in bulk. They'd sit on the shelf down in our basement. Those little things, the simple things in life, became important.

After I graduated from college, I left country life to work in the corporate world. I worked over thirteen years in the business and banking community at one of the largest banks in Kansas. Working my way up from being a teller to assistant vice president; I learned how to run a business and how to become involved with the local community, which has served me well.

During the same time, I had the opportunity to pursue one of my life's passions, training and showing horses professionally. I had always done it on the side and one day I decided I didn't want to be part of Corporate America anymore. I also knew that if I didn't take the opportunity to train and show horses, I would never know if I could hang with those "big time trainers" that I competed against. I left Corporate America, started training horses full time, and because I wanted to pursue my passion, I ended up in Texas.

After coming to Texas in 1988, I was very successful training and showing race horses and performance horses. While in Texas my husband and I were working for owners of National Champion Paint horses. About 4 months after we arrived in Texas the owners got transferred to Michigan. They wanted us to go with them, but we decided that Michigan was even colder than Kansas where we'd come from, so we didn't want to uproot and move to Michigan.

During my years training and riding horses, I knew that injuries were always a possibility. Well, I finally got bucked off a race horse, and broke my back in five places. At 33, I was finding that the ground that I sometimes connected with while riding horses was getting harder and harder.

Tapping back into my family's natural healthcare, I sought out and went to many chiropractors. The ones I went to in Texas all did the same type of adjustment: what I call "rack them and crack them". It wasn't the kind of chiropractic that I grew up with and was used to receiving. I had always gone to a chiropractor in Kansas who did a combination of chiropractic and acupuncture. That type of care was always effective for the injuries that I had suffered during the years.

After searching for that type of chiropractor for a while in Texas, someone finally said "Why don't you go see old Doc Black down in Mansfield?"

The day I had my appointment with Doc Black was one of those rare really cold and snowy days in Texas. I went to the appointment straight from the barn where I had been riding horses, so I had on my jeans, boots, chaps and spurs. I expected an older doctor, and when Doc Black walked out in holey blue jeans and cowboy boots, I immediately bonded with him. I knew I had found the right chiropractor.

But what I didn't know that first day was not only would I get back in shape, but the life journey I'm currently on would start. Shortly after I went to his practice, and the horse owners that we were training for left for Michigan, Dr. Black told me he needed a secretary receptionist. I agreed to fill in for a while, but after three weeks I confronted him and told him I didn't think he was looking for anybody else for the position. Of course, he said he hoped I wouldn't notice.

I knew from my business background that his office was a mess and could use someone to help him straighten it out, but I also knew from looking at his books that he couldn't afford me. We came to an agreement that after 90 days if I could help clean up and build his business that he would pay me a certain amount. Not only did I help build his business and revenue flow, but I also was hired to run his business.

At the time my ex-husband and I separated, and after working for Dr. Black for six months, we started dating each other. I accompanied him to seminars where I got to meet, and work with, some of the top healers and chiropractors from around the world. I actually got invited to sit in on workshop sessions and be part of the doctors practicing these different techniques. That's how I had the privilege to meet Dr. Victor Frank, who developed the Total Body Modification (TBM) technique. Dr. Frank took me under his wing and started telling me that he thought I needed to go to chiropractic school myself because he said I had "the gift of healing".

In 1989, Dr. Frank invited me to be part of a research seminar in Acapulco. I was the first non-doctor that he had ever invited to participate in this event. I became the first questor who was not a doctor, which means that I had gone through all of the different Total Body Modification (TBM) seminars that were available.

During that time, I had many very, very special people come into my life including Dr. Karl Parker. Dr. Karl was the son of Dr. Jim Parker, who actually started Parker College of Chiropractic, now Parker University, that's located in Dallas. Despite his encouragement to go to chiropractic school, I felt at 34 it was too late. But he encouraged me and I started my chiropractic training and studies at Park College of Chiropractic. In 1995 I had graduated from Parker with honors and immediately went into practice for myself while sharing space with two of Dr. Jim Parker's grandchildren, Dr. Rob and Dr. Kelly.

The first year in practice I learned a lot. With my chiropractic license at hand, I discovered that their plan was to give me space to practice and access to everything they had in their clinic, but they weren't going to pay me a salary. I would get paid a percentage of business I brought in: so if I had patients, I got paid and they got paid. But if I didn't have patients, I didn't get paid, none of us got paid.

That need drove me to work very hard to build my practice. A year later I felt I was ready to venture out on my own so with a small stack of patient files, I opened my own clinic. Today, that small stack of original patient files sit in my cabinet, but after 20 years our practice has grown into our well-known, and well-respected Health by Hands Wellness Center.

"One Stop Body Shop"

When I went out on my own, I dedicated myself to providing a whole body solution for my patients. As a result, today I can provide the care my patients need through the 40 different techniques I utilize. Most chiropractors only know one or two techniques well enough to practice, which won't help people meet their optimum healthcare needs.

When you visit my clinic -- Health by Hands Wellness Center-- you'll hear the words "One Stop Body Shop". And now—"Beyond Chiropractic".

No, this isn't a car repair shop. Our "repair shop" focuses on whole body healing that helps our patients reach optimum health and live a happy, healthy life.

Now you can use our analogy of a car repair shop to the methods you deploy to take care of yourself. Let's consider what you eat. If you don't eat the right food to fuel your body, like a car that has the wrong oil or gasoline in it, it won't run at optimum power…and can damage the car (i.e. your body).

Going back to my childhood and roots in holistic healthcare, I vowed to build a wellness center that not only provided chiropractic care, but acupuncture, nutritional counselling and other supportive techniques. Today the clinic also provides allergy and stress elimination, one of two BStrong4Life strength-building programs in Texas, and personalized weight-loss programs.

I've dedicated myself to learning those 40-plus techniques, so I could serve those people who have run out of hope that nobody else has been able to figure out. I call my brand of chiropractic as "eclectic chiropractic" because I mix and match all of these different techniques.

I believe in wellness care--not emergency care—so I look at the whole body, how everything that is bothering the person is inter-related, and then I use the mix of techniques that the person needs to get back to optimum health. My "low force" techniques are focused on accomplishing the desired outcome to get patients back to health through the best methods that work for them.

The basis of my foundational work is a technique called Sacro-Occipital Technique or SOT, which involves the relationship between the bones of the head, the cranium, and the rest of the body. It lends itself very, very well to helping people with chronic pain and figuring out those patterns that the body has set into place, --compensation patterns. SOT includes cranial work and temporal mandibular joint (TMJ) protocols. I'm one of only four Sacro Occipital Technique practitioners in Texas, and one of a handful across the country. People come from all over the U.S. to be treated by me.

I also use a technique called Neurological Organizational Technique (NOT), or pieces of it, that I find to be very useful in stabilizing people's bodies, and providing a foundation for rediscovered health by rehooking primitive reflexes, so their neurological systems work better. By utilizing these two main techniques, I found that my patients were getting better 50 percent faster.

In addition, I offer an allergy treatment program with immune enhancement technology that helps patients who suffer from year-round or seasonal allergies. While I have many older patients that face osteoporosis, I have the BStrong4Life system which helps strengthen bones while also providing sports training and conditioning. The system is designed to improve your balance, coordination, and stability regardless of your age or conditioning level. Used just once a week, it strengthens your muscles, bones, and spine!

The other technique I like to use is the LifeLine technique. It's a great technique that helps clear those emotional and physical roadblocks experienced during your life that is impacting your current health.

I have largely a wellness practice. I do consultations now not only in the clinic, but on Skype also. The internet has been great for being able to expand my ability to reach people and talk to people. I have patients from all over the United States that come and stay for a week, or two. We send them back, usually to a chiropractor or a wellness practitioner in their area, and they do very well by seeing us intermittently over the years.

I'm proud to have also successfully treated many autistic, special needs, and ADD/ADHD patients, and being regarded as one of the top prenatal care chiropractors in Texas. A mom myself, I understand how a soon-to-be mom and her newborn can benefit from chiropractic care during pregnancy and after birth.

It's been a great life. I love it. It's the only thing I've ever done in my life that I haven't been bored. You never know who's going to walk through the door, or what they're going to present me with. It's like getting to be a doctor and a friend and a detective all at the same time!

My Approach to Health and Wellness

Everyone – no matter how old or young you are – needs to be very proactive about their healthcare.

You need to be proactive about your wellness because if you get to the point where you need Western medicine, drugs or surgery, you're now in reactive mode to whatever degenerative situation, whatever state of "dis-ease" that your body has moved into.

The techniques that I use can pick up a dysfunction at about 5 to 10 percent, so they're perfect for those people that come in and say, "I just really don't feel well. I've been to my doctor. We've run all the blood tests. They all look normal. Nobody can figure out what's going on, but I know something isn't right." That's the best opportunity for people to take control, and find out about their bodies.

Let's go back to the analogy about a repair shop and cars. Our cars come with a manual. Our bodies didn't come with a manual attached to our ankles. At our "one stop shop" we help people write the specific manual that works for their bodies so that they can know how to be proactive and how to head off those situations before they become actual candidates for the western model of drugs and surgery.

You can always do drugs and surgery. There's always that option. But sometimes after you've had surgery, it's difficult to actually go back to a pre-surgery condition if you have recurring problems post-surgery. You can help improve quality of life. You can make them feel better, move better, think better, but it's really hard to get them back to where they might possibly have been prior to the surgery.

Here's a story about a new patient who didn't have just one, but multiple surgeries. I just started the new patient about three weeks ago who came in because he was having vertigo. We got rid of the vertigo almost immediately. But during our conversations I discovered that he had recently had knee replacement surgery. What's scary is after knee replacement surgery, he had a hospital-induced infection as a result of an injection and he quickly became septic. While in intensive care for two weeks, the knee rehab that he was supposed to going through was left by the wayside in lieu of trying to keep him alive.

While the knee didn't rehab well itself, when he was finished with rehab he found that he was numb from mid-calf down to his foot. He had a sensation of having a rock underneath his foot all of the time, and his knee was swollen, hot and collecting fluid.

Think that's bad, while doing his exam I also discovered he had a fusion at his cervical vertebra (C5-C6). Once a professional baseball player he felt a little sharp pain up in the top of his shoulder whenever he was pitching. They decided that because he had a little bit of degeneration in there at (C5-C6), they should go in and put a plate in that area and fuse those two joints together.

When I looked at his X-rays, I looked at him and I was like, "What kind of pain were you having before you had that surgery on your neck?" He said, "I was just having this little bit of pain on top of my shoulder." I said, "You didn't have any pain going down into your arm? You didn't have any tingling in your arms, your hands, your fingers?" He said, "No, I didn't have any of that. There was just this little thing and it hurt when I pitched and did overhead presses with weights, so they decided if they fused my neck it would go away."

Well, it did take care of that pain, but what I saw on my X-rays was that the symptoms I normally see in people that need a neck fusion surgery weren't there. He actually had perfect patency: the openings of where the nerves come out of the spine and go down to the different parts of the shoulder and to his arms, were perfectly open. He confirmed that by saying, "No, I didn't have any of that particular pain."

Likewise, he had a Lumbar fusion done several years ago. He had not experienced any radicular pain down his legs, but had a little bit of pain along one of his Sacroiliac joints, which is the joint between where your hip bone joins onto the triangular shaped bone at the end of your spine. Thy decided that he needed to have that fused so he has another piece of hardware down where the lumbar spine joins the sacroiliac joint (L5-S1). Once again this was a health issue that should have been treated conservatively before it became a surgical intervention.

When he came to see me for the vertigo it was actually the first time that he had ever had any chiropractic experience. There were a lot of things I believe that could have been done and accomplished without surgery for him, and he wouldn't have had to have the neck fusion. Now it's something that we can work around, but it's certainly a problem area. Because he doesn't have full range of motion in that area, now the body is forced to create a compensation pattern for it.

This patient's situation is a prime example that everyone has to be proactive about their wellness so they don't have to be reactive about their healthcare later on. In the United States, we are a system of insurance. Yes, I do file insurance for my patients if they have chiropractic coverage and benefits, however, I would prefer to work in that wellness model and not have to use any insurance because insurance does not see the need to keep people "well".

Most western doctors feel that they only have to treat what they see when you present to them. As a result, people end up on a lot of drugs. They end up on chronic pain management. They end up losing hope that they can have a full-quality life again. They also end up going down a path which sometimes there's no return. It's certainly not as easy to regain quality of life after going down that direction of drugs, surgery and chronic pain management. But it is a lot easier to be proactive about what you put in your body, what you drink, how you think, and how physically active you are. Remember: it's very important to keep moving because if you don't move it, you lose it.

Let me go back to what we eat. Why is diet so important to a healthy life? Here's the analogy about the car again: Your body is like a car. It will run as long as you provide fuel for it to run, and maintain it so it runs at its optimum level. If you think about food as your fuel, and alternative healthcare which is supportive as your maintenance, you'll have a healthier life. Think in terms of "eat to live" versus eating to satisfy an emotional need. And the quality of food is important too. Ask your alternative healthcare practitioner to help educate you on the types of foods that you should eat or research online sources for meals and information about the food groups. Again you want food that is pure, natural fuel for your body. Nothing that will make you sluggish or bog you down. Choose those foods that are not in boxes, bags or cans!

I want people to have the optimal quality of life that they can possibly have. I've been doing this long enough to know that there's no one magic bullet. I believe that you have to use a combination of different approaches, and work different parts of the body. It's a connection between the body, the mind, the spirit, and your biochemistry. All of those things have to play nicely with each other. We like to harmonize the body parts and the different aspects of healing together so that people are in a place where they are empowered to do better and be better.

You Are What You Eat and Drink

So what are the benefits of a healing program specific to your needs? The main benefit is that your nervous system continues to work well and serve you well.

Here comes the car analogy AGAIN. Let's just imagine you're driving down the street and your check engine light comes on, hopefully you're not putting a piece of duct tape over that check engine light and turning your radio up to overcome the rattles. You're actually going to take your car in and have it looked as if the check engine light comes on. But to make sure the check engine light doesn't come on again, you'll have your car's oil changed regularly, rotate your tires so your vehicle can serve you to the best of its ability.

Now let's go back to your body. A health care program will focus on keeping your body strong, and you being able to give it the quality fuel that it needs to run properly and without problems. As I said before, you are what you eat and drink. Let's start with something simple: you need to drink a minimum of a quart of water for every 50 pounds of body weight. Drink pure filtered water because tap water has all kinds of chemicals in it.

I quit drinking tap water when they hung a sign on my door that said, "Do not put your fish into tap water that you have just run because it will kill them."

It's easy to find out if a person drinks enough water. I use a lot of kinesiology and muscle testing in my practice, and if they haven't had enough water a muscle test will be very "squishy" or take longer to lock. I've discovered if they swish water in their mouth, the muscle test automatically locks. It's amazing how the body responds when a substance like water is introduced within the body's energy field. Muscle testing is a non-invasive way of evaluating the body's imbalances. The patient puts their arm out to the side and I apply slight downward pressure as the patient resists. If the patient is properly hydrated when I apply pressure the muscle will be strong and steady. If not hydrated patient would not have the strong steady response. So when I say the muscle "locks" I am referring to the strong steady response.

Water is one of the things that if I could get people to drink enough water every day for the rest of their lives, a lot of my business would go away. So many people think they don't like water for whatever reason: many because they grew up in an area where the water tasted bad. I know my grandparents and my aunt and uncle who lived in Oklahoma had so much sulphur in their water that it permeated the air like rotten eggs. Nobody wanted to drink that water. People drank tea, milk and all other kinds of things to cover up the taste and the smell of that water.

People that were in the military often times have been on water restrictions, and so they've learned to train their bodies to think that they don't need as much water. A lot of people that come out of the military and have had injuries or Post-Traumatic Stress Disorder (PTSD), even if they aren't water drinkers, they drink tons and tons of coffee. They drink alcohol. I'm not saying that those things in moderation are necessarily awful and bad-- a little bit of most things really isn't that detrimental to the body if you're doing all the rest of the things that you can do to the best of your ability.

Recently I came across structured water called H9. It's called the fourth phase of water because the molecules are very, very small allowing them to have the capacity to move easily across into the cell membranes. Let's visualize how it works: if you have a chain link fence and you take a softball and you throw it up against a chain link fence, what's going to happen? It's going to bounce off the fence, right? Then if you take a handful of BBs, and you throw those up against that chain link fence they're going to go through. That's the difference between regular water and this fourth phase of water.

There are three phases with regular water: liquid, gaseous and frozen. The fourth phase happens when the temperature is dropped just above freezing and a gelatinous water structure is created. Once they reach that phase, extra hydrogen molecules are infused in the gelatinous water structure. The result is water with a reduced molecular size, so it more easily crosses into the cell membranes. One bottle of H9 is about the equivalent of 5 or 6 bottles of the same size of regular filtered water.

Everyone has to remember that our bodies are 90% water. You have to put water in to replace the water lost through urination, sweating, processing foods we eat, and other bodily functions.

Another thing I have patients start is a sugar control diet. The sugar control diet eliminates all foods that have high glycemic indexes out of the diet for two to three weeks. This gives an opportunity for the liver and the pancreas, which communicate as far as your insulin regulation, to be able to rest a little bit. They also have to eat something every 2 hours. This tells the body that it's going to have a constant supply of food, nutrition and energy.

If patients don't understand the importance of sugar elimination, I will ask them if they have a pet if they would replace the pet's water with the tea or soda they drink. Most of them of course say "no" because their pet would die. That's when I ask what the difference between their pet and themselves is? I like to say "You should think as much of yourself as you do of your pets for sure."

I also tell my patients that, "You have to participate. We're really good at what we do here, but I can't follow you home. If you want to participate and you want to try a little, we'll all try a lot to support you in those efforts, but you really need to learn to participate."

Here's something that you can easily do: when you go food shopping, shop the outside aisles of your grocery store because that's where you find all of the natural things. Fruit and vegetables. Eggs. Nothing is in boxes, bags or cans.

The degeneration of people's health has degenerated since the 1920s when we as a country started eating lots of sugary treats. Right now the average person has an inordinate amount of sugar in their life during the course of a year. In my household, people come over and visit and they want a little sugar for their coffee. I inform that, "Except for Thanksgiving and Christmas when I do a little baking, we don't have sugar in this house. If you want it, you're going to either have to get it or you're going to have to use some of the sweetening substitutes that we use and believe in. We particularly like products like Xylitol and Erythritol. Those have low glycemic indexes. They taste good. They're teaspoon for teaspoon the equivalent of sugars. Some people like stevia and some people like a product called Lohaan I'm just starting to use and experiment with the Lohaan and some of my muscle testing. If people have a reaction to the xylitol, which can sometimes make them a little gaseous, they can almost always go and switch into its sister product called erythritol and not have those gastrointestinal issues that they might have with Xylitol.

It's about learning how to use those things that your body likes. I encourage my patients to be high maintenance when they go into a restaurant. Just because it doesn't say that, "This is what is included in your meal," ask for what you can get, what you can substitute. I have a favorite little breakfast place. It's one of those country Texas style breakfasts, country breakfasts with eggs, hash browns, waffles and pancakes. I ask them to do substitutions. I get a vegetable omelette. I want extra spinach. I love onions. My husband is not real crazy about that, but I love onions. Then I'll have them bring me a big dinner salad to go with my omelette. That's what I'll order for my breakfast. It has high protein. Doesn't have a lot of sugar in it, and keeps my energy high for a number of hours.

While at the clinic, I don't usually take a lunch and I don't take breaks. Once I start, I just go clear through the day. I used to take a lunch and what I found was I would try to work in patients that weren't on the schedule, but needed to be seen and then I wouldn't get a lunch. Then I would spend the afternoon mad because I hadn't had my lunch. Now we just set out plates of vegetables and fruit in the clinic. Our staff as well as the patients graze on this. We encourage everybody to help themselves if they're in the clinic and happen to walk by a plate of veggies. One of my staff's jobs is to make sure that I have food during the day and that there is a plate of something there that I can graze on.

I do a lot of smoothies. I do a lot of eggs, a lot of fish, protein, tuna fish, and wild caught salmon as part of my daily diet. Do I cheat? Absolutely. One of my very favorites is Mexican food. If I could, I'd probably eat Mexican food, chips and salsa, and queso dip seven days a week. I can't do that though because it's not good for my health— and having once weighed close to 200 pounds, I know I can put on weight very easily. I now maintain a weight of 125-130 easily.

I used to be extremely heavy so I have a special understanding for those people that have a weight problem. Unfortunately, the majority of our population these days is leaning toward either having a few extra pounds to being quite frankly obese. The fact that our children no longer go out and play, mainly because we can't turn them loose in the neighborhoods due to safety factors these days, means they don't get the physical exercise that they should get to stay healthy. Instead, they park themselves in front of television or video games.

Not only has the increase in playing video games at home or on cell phones resulted in children being heavier and less healthier, but I've actually seen a lot of what we call "text neck" and pain in wrists and fingers in kids.

I can't just say children are the only ones who need to stop playing games on their cell phones, but adults too need to put their phones down and stop texting, emailing or talking all the time. Next time you're at a restaurant just stop for a second and look around: what you see is everybody's head is down as they email or text on their phone, or even playing games or searching on the web. Another thing I like to share with my patients is what I do with my family when we go out to eat, we put our phones down, we put them on vibrate and we actually have a conversation. What a novel idea. Find out what we're doing and how we're feeling and what our plans for the day might be.

That's some of the things that I teach my patients. I think that they have to have tools that work and will fit into their lifestyle. You can't ask somebody to do something that doesn't work in their world because they may resent it. They may do it for a little while, but they certainly won't make it a life habit. It won't be a behavior modification thing. It has to be something that they enjoy and see a lot of benefit from and see that benefit early on. Most people change only because whatever benefit they're getting no longer outweighs the price that they're paying.

Albert Einstein said, "The definition of insanity is continuing to do what you've always done and expecting a different outcome." That's actually on my business cards.

That's one of the things that I drive home with my patients every day: if you want a different outcome than what you're currently experiencing then you need to make a choice, change your mind, take an action step, do one little thing every day or every week. If you think about it, if you change just one thing a month over the course of a year, you will change 12 things. If you're really motivated and you want to change something once a week, then you've got 52 things that you've changed over the course of a year. If you do that several years in a row, all of a sudden you find that you're a different person and your body performs differently for you.

Three Steps to Wellness

So far we've discussed one of the three steps to wellness.

One being **"you are what you eat and drink"**.

The second being **"you have to use it or lose it"**, which means you have to keep things in motion. You have to keep using your muscles. Your whole body is just a system of levers and pulleys which are your muscles and ligaments. If either of the levers or the pulleys aren't functioning, if they don't have free range of motion, if they're tight stiff, then that means they're not getting the proper stimulation in your nervous system. When that happens, things start shutting down.

Now, let me tell you about the third one: **thoughts become things. If you have bad thoughts, ultimately bad things will happen to your body.** I've been doing this long enough now to realize that a lot of problems that people have are negative emotional patterns that get stuck in their body's energy field, and as they go back into situations that trigger these different emotions, these different responses, what we find is that they have a lot of disease. They have a lot of sickness. They develop allergies. They can't digest their foods properly for a variety of reasons. Ultimately you are what you think, and what you think becomes you.

I want to go back to "use it or lose it". I've always been physically active but about three years ago I had X-rays and found out I had the beginning stages of some osteopenia or osteoporosis, which is loss of bone density. Being who I am, I knew that I wasn't going to take any of the osteoporosis drugs, so I started looking for natural solutions that would help me stop this tendency and actually move me into a place where my bones would become stronger, as I progressed.

Osteoporosis today is labelled as a silent killer. Most of the time found in the elder population, you'll hear about people over 60 who fall and break their hips. Actually what happens in many cases is that their bones have become so brittle because they've lost so much calcium out of their bones. Normally what happens is the person takes a step, twists, turns, the bone breaks and then they fall. Sadly, many times you'll then hear of someone who fell, broke their hip and then is dead in three weeks. For some reason a natural sequela of a fractured hip is that the person throws an embolism that ends up in their lungs or brain.

It's really important to keep your bones strong. You don't know that you're leeching calcium out of your bones unless you have what's called a bone density test. I recommend that every person now over the age of 40 should probably get one. Because of the nature of our diets, we have moved into creating an acid environment in our body and that acid environment, because our bodies are survival mechanisms, has to be buffered with something. Calcium has a very high alkaline Ph, so one of your body's first responses is that it pulls calcium out of your bones in an effort to buffer that acidity that's going on in your body.

When that happens over time, you become osteopenic, loss of bone density, or move into a state of osteoporosis. On the search to reduce my loss of bone density, I discovered a system called whole body vibration. Whole body vibration was developed in Russia. The Russians had found out that the cosmonauts who were in space for a long time, later experienced osteoporosis as a result of no gravity to act on their bodies for a period of time.

As a result, the Russians developed a system called whole body vibration. It's actually a platform that people stand on, and the vibrations actually cause the muscles and the fibers that attach into the bones to be stimulated and contract at about 40 to 60 times per second. If you think about that, that's really quite a lot of contraction going on in a short period of time. The system has evolved since it was first discovered in Russia. There's now a number of these whole body vibration units.

I actually use a whole body vibration system called Power Plates. A lot of the professional sports teams have them in their training facilities because we call it "exercise on steroids". About 15 to 20 minutes on a Power Plate is the equivalent of 45 minutes to 60 minutes of exercise in a gym. Anything that you can do on the floor in a gym, whether it's with weights, stretching, hand weights, or resistance bands, you can do that exercise on the whole body vibration unit, and exponentially increase your results.

Another machine I use for myself and my patients is the Biodensity machine. It has pressure plates on it that measure forced pounds of pressure in different positions. There's a chest press, a leg press, a pull down, and a vertical lift. These are all motions that we use on a daily basis, things that we need to keep our core strong. What we have found through different trials and studies is that by using the equipment 15 to 20 minutes once a week, a person can actually rebuild bone density at the rate of something between five to thirteen percent per year. In the past, the only alternative a person had to stop osteoporosis is by taking drugs.

I know it's easy for me to talk about the equipment, but let me tell you a story about one of my favorite patients who used the Power Plates.

About two years ago, a man walked in the front door holding a piece of paper. He said "I'm looking for Dr. Kathi." I happened to be there walking through the lobby and I said, "You just found her because I'm Dr. Kathi." He said, "My son says I need to come and see you." I said, "Okay, what do you need to see me for?" "Well I had 2 hips replaced, and my son is a Rolfer," he said. (A Rolfer is someone who does body work on a very deep intense level.) "He was working on me and he said my hips aren't level and my sacrum needs to be adjusted and that I need you because you do soft easy techniques because you won't hurt my hip replacements."

He handed me the piece of paper which was an email from his son and it starts out by saying, "Dad, you're 92 years old. You need some special care, and I think I found a lady that can help you."

I dropped the paper and said, "You're 92 years old?" He went, "Yes." I said, "Well you're really pretty amazing for 92."

What I didn't know at the time was that his balance was becoming more and more dangerous for him to be walking around. He was using a cane. His hands had become so stiff that he couldn't button his shirt. He actually would go across the hall in his independent living center and knock on the door of the lady that lived across the way, and have her button his shirts for him. He couldn't work his fingers well enough to tie his shoes so he was wearing exclusively tie on shoes with a Velcro closing across them. He fatigued very easily.

His name is Mr. Hank and I ended up seeing him as a patient. I adjusted him by using a technique called Activator, which is a very soft easy technique which he really resonated with it. We also started working him out on the Power Plates.

To help with his stability, I'd have him go out and rest his fingers on a railing, keep his eyes up, and walk up and down the hallways. What we found was that by doing that and shifting his vision, that it automatically had him come straighter, stand straighter and move his head back over his shoulders.

We come into the world in a fetal position. If you ever notice with elderly people, they have a tendency to return to that fetal position. Their head comes forward. They get that little humpy thing on their back. Your head weighs about 10 or 12 pounds, so if you think about hanging your head off your shoulders like this, and you're always looking down at your feet, the natural tendency is going to be to lose your balance and fall down ultimately.

When Mr. Hanks first started coming in to the clinic, he couldn't step up on the Power Plate which is about 10 to 12 inches tall. We used a little platform, and divided it up into two steps for him. After about 2 months, he was able to step up on the step by himself. He was carrying his cane, but he wasn't using it much. What we found within another few months was that he came in and he was so excited because he said, "I buttoned by own shirt today." That's when we found out that he hadn't been able to do that for a very long time. It's those little things of using your body and giving it the proper stimulation, continuing to use it that will keep you strong for a very long time.

In Mr. Hank's honor as well, he weighs between 165 and 170 pounds. He's always been very cognitive of his diet and his food. If he gains up toward 170, he goes on soup and protein and drops it back down to 165. In the last 35 years, he has never varied more than those 5 pounds. It's been a struggle to get him to drink water because he says, "If I drink more water, I'm always in the bathroom." We're like, "Well, better out than in, and you don't want to stop everything up. Besides that, when you have to get up and go to the bathroom you have to move." He actually now also keeps a resistance band hanging off his chair.

Some words of wisdom that I'll pass around. Mr. Hank just celebrated his 95th birthday. He feels well enough now that he's golfing once a week. He takes an art class. He comes over here and works out twice a week. He's just the most wonderful man. If you look at pictures of him that we had back when he came in two and a half years ago versus now, he looks like he has dropped 20 years off his life. He doesn't watch a lot of TV. He reads a lot. He was a retired engineer and in Sr. Management at Vought Aircraft Manufacturing, where he was involved in some of the pilot programs for some of the military planes. He still has a great interest in old military planes and aircraft manufacturing.

One of the other things that he does is that he always makes a list every day. He puts more on his list that he can possibly get done because that way, he says, he'll have something to do tomorrow. I think that's wise for everybody to keep some projects going, and keep your list. Keep some things out there that you want to do and make sure that you're working toward those things. I think that keeps hope and happiness in your life and gives you a function, something to get up for every morning. Then you can decide what those action steps are you're going to take on whatever was left on your list from yesterday.

Taking Care of Your Physical Body...and Mind

We're a society of flexion. Everything we do any more is in front of us unless we actually make a concerted effort to strengthen our extensor muscles and our back muscles. I know: I bend over patients all day.

We all need to learn how to stretch, and do things to strengthen our back muscles, to bring our head back over our shoulders. We completed a series of videos which includes a first visit with a patient, consultation techniques, Neurological Organizational Techniques (NOT), which turns on all the switches in your body that reconnects the neurology and the primitive reflexes.

As I say, use it or lose it. At the very least, get up stretch, move. If you have an office job, you need to make sure that you're getting up once in a while and moving into a position that is going to be different than how you've been sitting there for hours.

I've been talking with people about Sitting Equals Smoking: The Next Ultimate Health Hazard. When you think about it, the repercussions of what happens when you sit a lot, is it increases the potential for cardiovascular disease. It increases the potential for arthritis, for pain, for headaches, for all kinds of different ailments. It's one of the easiest things to fix. You've just got to get up once in a while. You've got to move.

I tell people get some resistance bands, take them to your office, and leave them in the break room. Let everybody in the break room have access to them. Put them in a place between you and the bathroom so when you go to the bathroom or get a drink of water, you'll be able to pick it up and do a few stretches.

Another simple thing to do: There's a doorway going into another room almost everywhere so you can actually go into a doorway, put your hands up on it, stretch back and just do push ups in the doorway. Make sure you bring your head back over your shoulders because it's probably been hanging out there looking at something in front of you for a while. That in of itself will open you up: it'll stretch our pec muscles. A great way to stretch is to imagine that you are just bringing your shoulder blades together and hold that position for a little bit. Then relax it, and go back again, and hold it and relax.

If you do that multiple times throughout the day, ultimately you will feel much better at the end of the day. I'm fortunate. I have some Power Plates in the back room, so at the end of my day I go get on the Power Plate for 10 or 15 minutes and suddenly that 45 minute drive I have going to the country is a lot more doable because my blood's circulating. I'm waking up. I just feel a lot better when I get home and I'm in a better mood for my husband when I get there.

I'm going to move away from discussing stretching, and address the emotional side of healing.

Since 2001 I've had dogs in my clinic. Sometimes I think that people don't come to see me but they come to see my dogs. It's been great because they truly are therapy dogs. My little Italian greyhound always shows up when we're in LifeLine sessions. Sometimes he puts his paw up on people's hands and my arm and then tries to help us muscle test. If people are really in good moods, he's crazy about playing ball. If they're really down, he sits next to them and lets them pet him.

I have a new puppy that's a Goldendoodle. He is in training to be a therapy dog. He's amazing. He is the most chilled out puppy that I have ever been around. He's been really easy to train. Everybody loves him. His name is Cabo.

I have a theory that if people come to my clinic, I want to set the energy as being more of a home, family environment, some place where people can come and be comfortable. I think that's important in your healing process. I think too many people go into doctor's offices where they are formal and everybody is dressed the same and everybody has an attitude of, "You're not going to get that much better. We can just work you with drugs or this or that." We really like to set an environment where it feels like home. A lot of times when people get done with their treatments here and they're on their maintenance programs, if they're in the neighborhood, they'll just stop in and just say hi because they say, "We just like it here."

Transforming Your Health Through LifeLines

My favorite thing to talk about is the relationship between how to think—and what to think about—as it impacts your overall health

We hear that in all the positive motivation seminars that you are what you think. You have to change your thoughts, because by changing your thoughts, you change your actions. However, the body is one of those, like I said, "survival" pieces of equipment. The body's main job and the subconscious' main job is to protect your spirit, no matter what the cost of the other systems in the body.

I've been working with different kinds of neuro-emotional clearing techniques during the 20 years that I've been in practice. I started out with a technique called Neuro Emotional Technique that was developed by Scott Walker, who is a chiropractor out in California. From that I've evolved into a number of other things. Right now my very favorite is a technique called LifeLine. It was developed by a doctor named Dr Darren Weissman. Dr Weissman and I both practiced a similar kind of chiropractic prior to the time that he developed LifeLine.

Back in 2007 I had heard about LifeLine several times. I got some literature from Dr Weissman about an upcoming seminar in Chicago. I was scheduled to teach a four-hour workshop at a seminar in Dallas with Dr. Karl Parker. But I kept dreaming that I was meant to go to the LifeLine seminar in Chicago. I called Dr. Karl said, "I would not do this unless I thought it was really important. I am really feeling the need to go to a LifeLine seminar in Chicago, the weekend that you're having a seminar. Do you think that you could find somebody else to fill that 4 hour slot for me?" He said, "I know you, and if you feel that strongly about being there, if I have to go in and teach that class myself, I'll go." We hugged and I said, "Thank you and I love you." I purchased my ticket to go to the LifeLine seminar in Chicago.

As I had discussed before because of my involvement with horses and thee fractures in my back, when I go to seminars, I tend to sit on the edge toward the back so I can stand up, sit down, move around, and stretch a little bit during the seminar. I'm not used to sitting all day because at the clinic I'm on my feet seven or more hours a day. I don't sit down a lot. When I do sit down, I use a balance ball, which is great for my back. I encourage everybody if you haven't checked out a balance ball to use for a chair, you should do that.

Another thing I want to tell you before I continue about the LifeLine seminar in Chicago, is share one of main events in my past. I had a granddaughter—Daxton--who was killed in a car accident when she was 2 and a half. Through all of my different modalities of healing and work and emotional clearing, I really thought I had a pretty good handle on that and that I had processed the grief. She was a daily part of my life. She was a great little girl. Big smile on her face. Really wise beyond her years. She talked sentences when she was about 14 months old. She was a daily presence at the clinic.

My daughter was one of my massage therapists, so Daxie would come to work and also help out at the front desk with the office manager, Tracy. If the front desk person was dealing with somebody's insurance and trying to tell that insurance company they needed to send our check right away, Daxton would go up and pat Tracy on the leg and would say, "Go easy Trace, go easy Trace. They're okay."

It was a huge loss to us when we lost Daxton in that car accident. Like I said, I thought I had a pretty good handle on it.

Anyway we're about midway through the first day and Dr. Darren says, "Is there anybody here who has any back pain?" I held up my head, and he said, "Well come on down here." He started to work on me, while describing my pain and applying this LifeLine technique. Daxton…the accident….and my grief started to surface.

LifeLine is one of those techniques that you don't have to say what's on your mind. You just have to connect with it and let the facilitator know that you've connected with something. Dr. Darren was not aware of anything that was going through my mind or what will come up for me, so we continue through the LifeLine process.

That night in my room I knew I had experienced something that I had never experienced before and felt renewed grief over the loss of Daxton. The next morning when I went back to the seminar I was still in that spot of grieving. The LifeLine practitioners just gathered me up and did the next step and the next step. By mid-day Sunday, I felt like the weight of the world had been lifted off my shoulders. I had renewed energy. I looked in the mirror and that hollow look that I'd had in my eyes for all of those years was gone.

I knew that was why I was supposed to be in Chicago that weekend. I also knew that I needed to become a Certified LifeLine practitioner just as quickly as I could.

Over the next 6 months, I kept returning to Chicago and became a Certified LifeLine practitioner in October 2007. I am one of 4 certified practitioners at this time in the State of Texas. I see miracles all the time doing LifeLine. I think it's a wonderful technique. It's about fourteen different techniques that's imbedded into one technique. It uses kinesiology, plus the five-element theory of Chinese medicine and how the interaction of all of the elements has to be in balance and flowing properly so the body can function.

When using the LifeLine technique, you will discover holding patterns in the subconscious mind. About 90 to 98% of everything that has ever happened to us is stored back there in the subconscious mind. Some of it's done just because we couldn't stand all of that sensory stimulation of everything hitting us at once. Some of it is done because we don't have the tools and resources at the time to be able to deal with things so it preserves our spirit by sectioning it over there or putting it into this little compartment. Sometimes it gets to come out and sometimes we pass from this world and it's still in those little boxes. Sometimes it stays in the boxes and is complicated by other things and those patterns get stuck in different parts of the body. We call them expression channels in LifeLine. Those expression channels can be emotional, structural, biochemical. Emotions can get stuck in those expression channels

Dr. Bruce Lipton, who is a cell biologist, did a lot of research on how cells react to their environment. What he found was that you could actually take the DNA, the nucleus out of the cell and the cell would continue to live, but it was dependent upon the environment it was in. Did it have a good medium to grow in? Was it healthy? Was it not?

Dr. Masaru Emoto did a lot of research and demonstrations showing how the power of just words placed on containers of water changed the crystalline structure of the water. He discovered that the crystals formed were beautiful if the words were in response to feelings like peace, hope, gratitude or love. However the water took on a very ugly, dark crystalline structure if heavy metal music was played, or words like hate, rage, or despair were put on the containers of water. We know that the frequency of words and symbolism has a lot of power within our bodies and leaves an imprint on our energy field.

LifeLine, like I said, has about 14 different techniques. It has some NeuroLinguistics Programming (NLP) embedded into it. It also has some eye movement release techniques (EMDR). The premise behind that is that sometimes when different things happen to you that your eyes were in a certain position at the time that event happened. Whenever your eyes go into that position it may trigger some of those neuro responses that you had and bring back that event.

We buy Kleenex by the case here because people do a lot of clearing, and it's a safe place for people to do that. When they're in the midst of crying, I won't touch them because in NeuroLinguistics Programming (NLP), touching somebody when they're at the height of an emotion will allow an "anchor" to be set. The next time somebody comes along and touches them in that same way, it would trigger that response of that grief or that sadness that they're in at that time. I wait until after they get done processing the emotion and then say something to bring out a smile or give them a hug at that point in time. Then I touch them and anchor those good feelings into them. Also embedded into LifeLine is the chakra system, which includes all of the body's energy centers; and quantum physics about how we're all connected energetically through the threads of the energy from the earth.

There's been a lot of studies that say that we can affect the thoughts of people on the other side of the world. We're all connected by this thread, this quantum energy field. We have the capability to tap into that quantum energy field through LifeLine.

As we go through LifeLine, the universal sign for "I Love You" is used to clear emotions that may come up during the session. Instead of touching the person. I just put my fingers up in front of them using the sign for "I Love You" and say, "Infinite Love and Gratitude. Infinite Love and Gratitude. Infinite Love and Gratitude."

The whole premise is that nothing negative can live in a field of unconditional love, so by collapsing those patterns that we've tapped into and surrounding it with that field of unconditional love, we can shift and change that energy. We can do it immediately. When I first start working with people I do a demonstration. Often times, I'll do this on their first visit just to let them know that sometimes their thinking is part of what is keeping them in that place of dis-ease in their body. I'll have them hold up an arm and I'll do a muscle test. I'll have them think of something that makes them very, very happy. I don't even want to know what that thought is. I just want them to THINK their happy thought. I do another muscle test. What we find is that their muscle will remain very strong. It will lock. Sometimes if a person is really big, it's like I could almost hang off of it and not budge that arm.

Then I'll ask them to think of something that makes them sad… a huge stress in their life…or something they don't like to think about. They'll think about that and just immediately when they do, I'll say, "Hold." I'll do their muscle test and in many cases, it just falls down. Then I'll say, "Okay, go back to your happy thought." We'll test again and it's strong. "Go to your sad thought," and immediately goes weak. That's how quickly your body's neurology can change just based on how you think. If you don't change the way your body responds to those thoughts, obviously you're not going to change the situation. You're not going to make it go away, but you can change your body's response to it.   Instead of reacting to the negative, you can stop step back a little bit, take a couple of breaths and act in a different manner that's going to support feeling better having that happier thought.

The emotional clearing techniques that I do actually will shift the body from where it has that weak muscle response. We associate that weak muscle response with either elements or emotions that we know are part of those elements. For instance, the Chinese medicine element wood has several emotions, primarily anger, frustration and resentment.

Also the various organs within the body associate with different emotions. The spleen and the pancreas have relationships to low self-esteem, lack of control, and bitterness. The pancreas, having to do with sugar regulation, will lose its "sweetness" if the person has a lot of bitterness in their life. That can actually drive those responses which can be the precursors to diabetics.

The stomach has issues such as vulnerability, abandonment, lost connections, and lost people. Lungs are grief and sadness, yearning. The bladder and the kidneys, they're a water element. Their main emotion is one that is fear The main bladder emotion is an emotion called pissed.

During LifeLine, we go through an entire protocol to collapse those feelings. At the end of the sessions, we find that those things that people think about that previously made them weak; they're now able to maintain strength. In that strength, they can make changes both in their hearts, minds, spirit and bodies. They will also be able to make better choices. They can "act" rather than "re-act".

A lot of the self-sabotage that we go through is because of emotional patterns, things that have happened in the past, which limits our belief systems. Those are those things that are placed into our minds, into our subconscious, into our energy field by people around us. Those are the thoughts and the things that people say, "What are you thinking about? You'll never do that. You're not good enough. You shouldn't do that." Those are all those things that if we hear them often enough and at a time when we're very impressionable and we haven't developed our own sense of self-worth, that they live in our bodies and in our minds and our subconscious sometimes forever.

It's very helpful to be able to take those things and shift those belief systems making people more likely to overcome those areas of self-sabotage, inability to complete things, inability to have good relationships. It's said that sometimes we marry people that are like our fathers and our mothers. Sometimes that's a good thing. More often than not, I find that sometimes that has some holes in it and some of those things that draw you to that other person because it reminds you of your mother or your father should probably be shifted a little bit and looked at with a different perception.

I've watched miracles happen right before my eyes while I've been doing LifeLine sessions. I had a teenager come to me right after I started doing the advanced work. The way that I found about her was she had actually come to an appointment with her brother several days before that. She was sitting out on the coach in the waiting room when I walked out. It appeared that she had a rope burn across the middle of her neck right here. I asked her. I said, "What happened to your neck?"

She was sixteen years old, so she was embarrassed by my questions. She said it was something that came up every summer. "Oh, it's not a burn or anything? Can I look at it?" It turns it was this raised mole that was about an inch wide and went from underneath one ear over to other ear. I ask her, "How long have you been having that?" She said, "It started about 4 years ago." She said, "Every year in the summer when I start getting out in the sun, it comes back." I was like, "Hmm, that's really interesting that it goes away in the winter and it comes back in the summer. I'm doing this new technique and I need somebody that I can practice on with some of this advanced work. Would you want me to practice on you and see if maybe we can do something with that, maybe make it not come back in the summer time?"

She and her mother agreed to my doing the LifeLine and scheduled a time for the following week. We started down the path of her LifeLine and discovered that this mole was the result of a generational pattern that was created out of anger, conflict and rage, from her father's side of the family. It was actually her father's grandfather. We had the capacity to trace back into generations sometimes if we have a need to do that, and as we were going through all of these different aspects on the flow chart of her LifeLine, I'm watching in amazement as the mole is going away.

I kept looking at it fading before my eyes. When she asked what I was looking at I told her to go down the hall and look in the mirror. All of a sudden I heard her scream. She said "It's gone. What did you do? It's gone." I said, "I don't know. I just did LifeLine like I've been told to do it and miracles happen. Sometimes Dr. Darren says that symptoms are gifts in strange wrapping papers." I explained what had happened, during the session, to her mother and we were finished. By that time, the mole was literally almost gone. To this date, it's never come back.

The long and the short of it is that her mother went and talked to her father, who told them that his grandfather had actually been a horse thief. What happened? The people became angry with him.....and hung him. Another part of this story, was the mole first appeared when she was living with her father and her stepmother. They had gotten into a huge fight. They had packed up her things, drove her to her mother's house, put her and her luggage out on the sidewalk and had driven off. There was a whole lot of rage, anger and revenge that was caught in that generational energy field and dumped through him onto her. All of that negative energy manifested on to her as the mole across her neck which came up just within a matter of days of them having gone off and left her.

Another time I had a lady call me who said, "I need for you to do a LifeLine. I heard some really great things about it." I was like, "Okay." I said, "What were we going to work on?" She says, "I have ovarian cancer and I'm going to have surgery tomorrow and I just want to make sure that I'm in as good a place as I can be to go into that procedure." I said, "Okay, that makes sense" (and thought to myself— "could we have had a bit more lead time to do this?"

The lady came in with her partner, and we all three discussed issues that come up surrounding ovarian cancer, emotions and family issues. She was scheduled for surgery the next morning to remove two tumors: one the size of an orange, and the other the size of a grapefruit. She had all of her diagnostic workups done earlier in the week so they knew pretty much what they were going to find when they went into do this surgery. When the surgeon went in the next morning, the tumor that was the size of the orange was gone and the tumor that was on the other side had been reduced to about half. Was LifeLine responsible? I can't say for sure. However, that's the only thing that we did differently. I do know that changing the energy of anything and raising the vibration on that creates a state where healing becomes possible.

There's all kinds of things like that that I experience with LifeLine-- besides my own personal experience with it. Now what I find LifeLine for me has become is, that if I get in a situation or see myself running a pattern of some sort, I immediately call one of my LifeLine friends. I have a very favorite friend that lives in North Carolina. We do Skype sessions back and forth on each other. I'll go, "Hey, Nikki, I don't want to be here for any longer. We need to do this. We need to shift this." I know that I don't have to stay in that place of having negative emotions or feeling badly. I can move through that, and I move through it very quickly.

I love doing the LifeLine Technique with people that have been through a lot of therapy because they already know what their issues are. It's really easy to tap into their energy and emotions, and just start shifting and moving energy out of the parts of their body where it might be stuck at. That's the whole thing is-- don't get stuck where you're at because there's always a LifeLine, a path to where you can go-- that's a better place than where you are.

LifeLine doesn't mean you have to be sitting next to each other. I and other practioners utilize Skype for LifeLine sessions. Right now there are over 300 practitioners worldwide.

Infinite Love and Gratitude

Every day when you get up, there's something so simple, yet so powerful, that you can do. It's connecting yourself to your energy field.

I do it every morning and what I have found is if I do it before I start seeing patients that things just flow better. I have what I call my "little voice" that sits over here behind my right shoulder. It chatters to me while I'm working and gives me insights and puts thoughts in my head that says, "Do this. Try this." It's interesting how often times I'll ask somebody about something and they'll go, "How did you know that? I was just thinking about that." This "hook up" process enhances that "connection" to be able to do those things.

So let me walk you through the process:

The first thing I want you to do is I want you to take 5 fingers together and put them right on top of your head. We're going to call that your Spirit point.

Then you're going to take your other hand and touch your chest. That's your Body point.

We're going to connect your Body and your Spirit and we're going to say, "Infinite love and gratitude. The connection of Body and Spirit. Infinite Love and Gratitude. The connection of the physical to the Spirit that lasts forever. Infinite Love and Gratitude. Infinite Love and Gratitude. Infinite Love and Gratitude."

Now.. I want you to pick your hand up from the top of your head and then I want you to put it right back down on top of your head because we're also going to connect your Body to your Spirit as well as your Spirit to your Body.

Say "Infinite Love and Gratitude of the connection of the Body and the Spirit. Infinite Love and Gratitude. Infinite Love and Gratitude."

Now I'm going to have you take your hand off the top of your head and off your chest.

On the count of 3, we're going to touch together. 1, 2, 3, touch. Touch Body and Spirit points at the same time.... There you go. We're going to unify your Body and your Spirit.

Say "Infinite Love and Gratitude to the unification of the physical Body and the Spirit. Infinite Love and Gratitude. Infinite Love and Gratitude. Infinite Love and Gratitude."

Now I want you to disconnect from those points and I want you to put your hand over your forehead. That is your Mind point which allows you to think. It's your mind that allows you to process information.

Now I want you to take your other hand and put it right on top of your head because we're going to connect your Mind to your Spirit.

Say "Infinite Love and Gratitude. Connection of the Mind and the Spirit. Infinite Love and Gratitude. Infinite Love and Gratitude. Infinite Love and Gratitude. Infinite Love and Gratitude."

Now I want you to take your hand off of your Spirit point on top of your head and touch your body because we're going to connect your Mind to your Body. We're going to hook up those thoughts that you have to your body. All of those physical aspects of your being.

Say "Infinite Love and Gratitude of the connection of Mind to Body. Infinite Love and Gratitude. Infinite Love and Gratitude. Infinite Love and Gratitude."

Once again, we want to unify this field between the Body and the Mind so take your hand off and take your hand off your chest. Now put both hands back down together, 1, 2, 3 and touch, because we're going to unify and harmonize that field, that connection between the Body and the Mind.

Say "Infinite Love and Gratitude of the harmonization of the body and the mind. Infinite Love and Gratitude. Infinite Love and Gratitude. Infinite Love and Gratitude."

Now take one finger and point it down toward the floor because underneath that floor is Mother Earth. Imagine you are all warm and snuggy and hugged in the arms of Mother Earth.

Say "Infinite Love and Gratitude to the connection of Mother Earth. Infinite Love and Gratitude."

Now I want you to take those 5 fingers that we used in the beginning and put them back on top of your head on your Spirit point because we're going to connect Mother Earth to your Spirit.

"Infinite Love and Gratitude to the connection of Mother Earth to your spirit. Infinite Love and Gratitude. Infinite Love and Gratitude. Infinite Love and Gratitude."

Now take your hand off of your Spirit point, off the top of your head and put it back over your forehead because we're going to connect Mother Earth to your Mind.

Say "Infinite Love and Gratitude of the connection of Mother Earth to your mind. Infinite Love and Gratitude connecting Mother Earth being grounded, rooted and Mother Earth connected to the soil, connected to the Earth, to our Mind. Infinite Love and Gratitude. Infinite Love and Gratitude. Infinite Love and Gratitude."

Take your hand off your forehead and touch your body because we also have to connect Mother Earth to your Body.

Say "Infinite Love and Gratitude of the connection of Mother Earth to the body. Infinite Love and Gratitude. Infinite Love and Gratitude. Restoring the connection of Mother Earth to the body. Infinite Love and Gratitude."

I want you to put your hands in prayer position. This is also one of the positions that you've seen people use when they say Namaste'. This is your connection to God's source, that higher being that "Higher Power" that you believe in, whatever that might be.

I want you to take your hands and put them on top of your head because we're going to connect Spirit to your Source and God.

Say "Infinite love and gratitude. Infinite love and gratitude to the connection of Source and Spirit. Infinite love and gratitude of the energy to that connection of Source. Coming into your Spirit which is eternal. Infinite love and gratitude. Infinite love and gratitude."

I want you to take your hands and put them right in front of your forehead because that's your mind. We're going to connect that power of sourcing God to your mind.

Say "Infinite love and gratitude of the connection, the power, the Source of God, Source to your Mind, to your thoughts. Infinite love and gratitude. Infinite love and gratitude. Infinite love and gratitude.

Now take that connection, that Source in God connection, and move it down in front of your chest, in front of your body. Again we're connecting God and Source to the Body, to your physical being, to that place that you've been given to live.

Say "Infinite love and gratitude. Infinite love and gratitude. Infinite love and gratitude. Infinite love and gratitude."

Surrounded by Infinite Love and Gratitude, nothing negative can live in this field.

…Reach out and touch someone. Let someone know that you love them, that you forgive them and that you have gratitude for every day that you're here.

Infinite love and gratitude!!!!

A Message from Dr. Kathi

No matter where you're located or when you need information about our integrated healing techniques, information about Health by Hands and Dr. Kathi is available 24/7.

Visit our YouTube channel: Health by Hands Wellness Center to learn more about our techniques, and Be Strong 4 Life.

Also visit our web site @:www.healthbyhandswellness.com to learn more about our services.

If you need to reach us by phone or email we'll get back with you as soon as possible!

Health by Hands Wellness Center

2510 Little Road

Arlington, Texas 76016

Phone: 817.930.0600

Fax: 817.451.1252

Email: drk@drkathi.net

http://healthbyhandswellness.com/

We completed a series of videos which includes a first visit with a patient, consultation techniques, Neurological Organizational Techniques (NOT) which we did all switches that reconnect the neurology and the primitive reflexes.

I work with people that have closed head injuries so we did a segment on that. We had a whole bunch of footage of parents, kids, adults that have been my patients doing testimonials. I have a couple of dogs in my clinic. You might have seen one walk through the background a while ago. I've always had dogs in my clinic since about 2001.